Feeding at Night

Written by
Jill Atkins

Ransom

At night, it is dark.

If we look up,
we might see the moon.

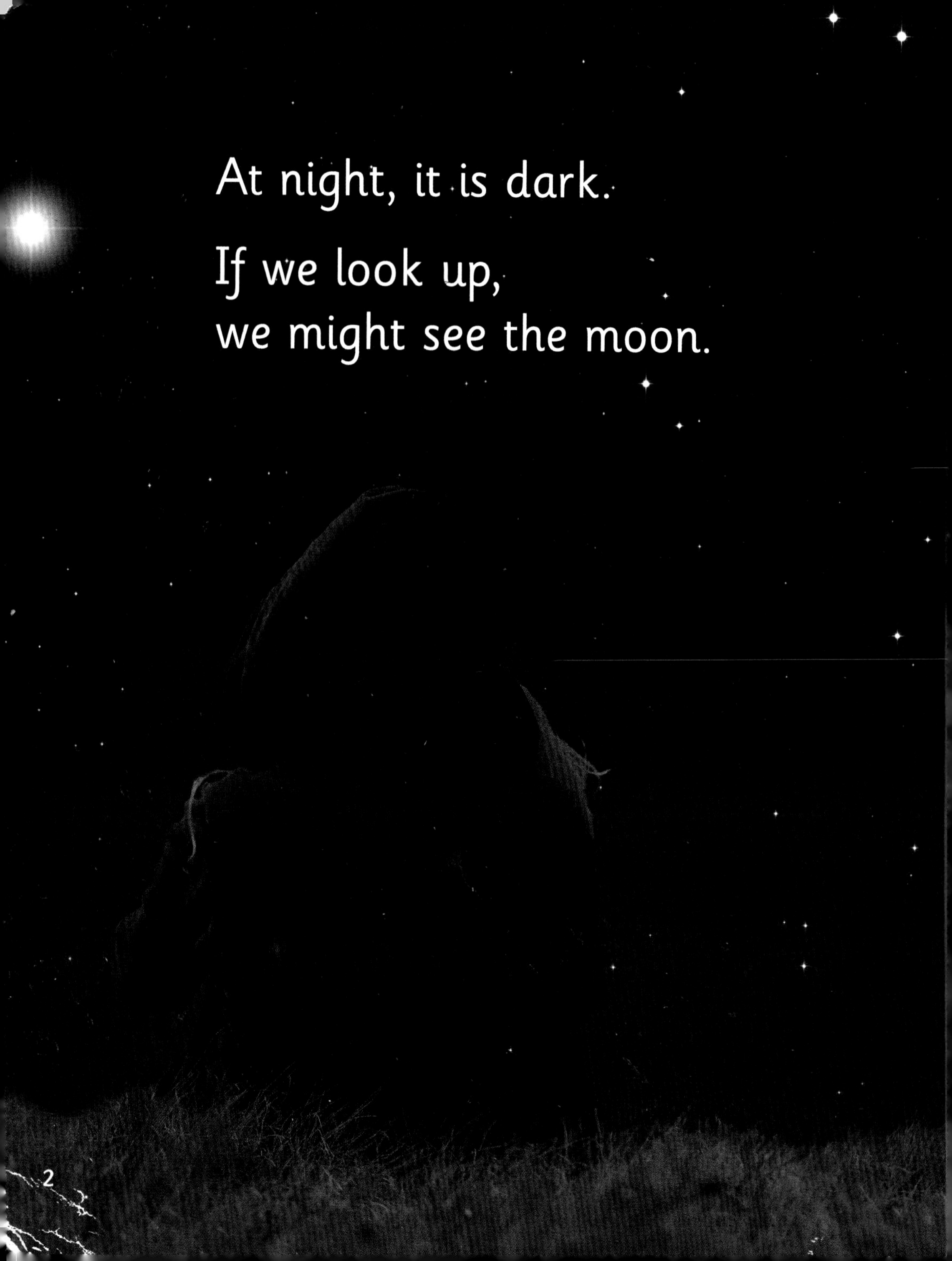

At night, the moon can seem near.

It lights up the darkness.

Owls go to bed in the light and look for food at night.

They are **nocturnal**.

An owl has sharp talons
and good sight.

It can see its food in the dark.

This is a barn owl.

This owl has
sharp ears.

We can hear this owl
hooting in the woods.

This is a bat.

It is hanging in a dark corner of a barn.

Bats are nocturnal, too.

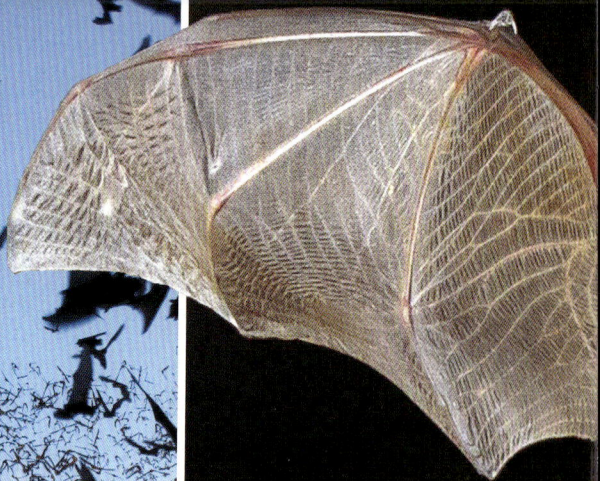

Bats zig-zag up and down, high in the dark air.

They feed on bugs for supper.

They cannot see well,
but they can hear well.

They can "see" with big ears.
This is sonic hearing!

The fox is nocturnal too.

This fox is in town at night.

He needs to look for food too.

As the sun gets up
in the morning, it gets light.

Then the owls and bats go to
bed – until it gets dark.